# From the Author

I absolutely LOVE Astronomy!
I think it is very interesting and I know you will feel the same way.

As you read through this book, practice saying all of the words.
You are going to be SUPER SMART, learning about the Solar System!

I personally love to draw and doodle so I included extra pages
in the back for your mind to create. Enjoy!

Check out the winner of the Art Competition, Benny Rodriguez, on page 2!
I also included the 6 runners-up because we really enjoyed their artwork too!

Check online to enter the art competition for the next book.
www.SuperSmartScienceSeries.com

**Share this series with your friends.**
**help them become SUPER SMART like you!**

-April Chloe Terrazas

**this SUPER awesome Book Belongs to:**

______________________________

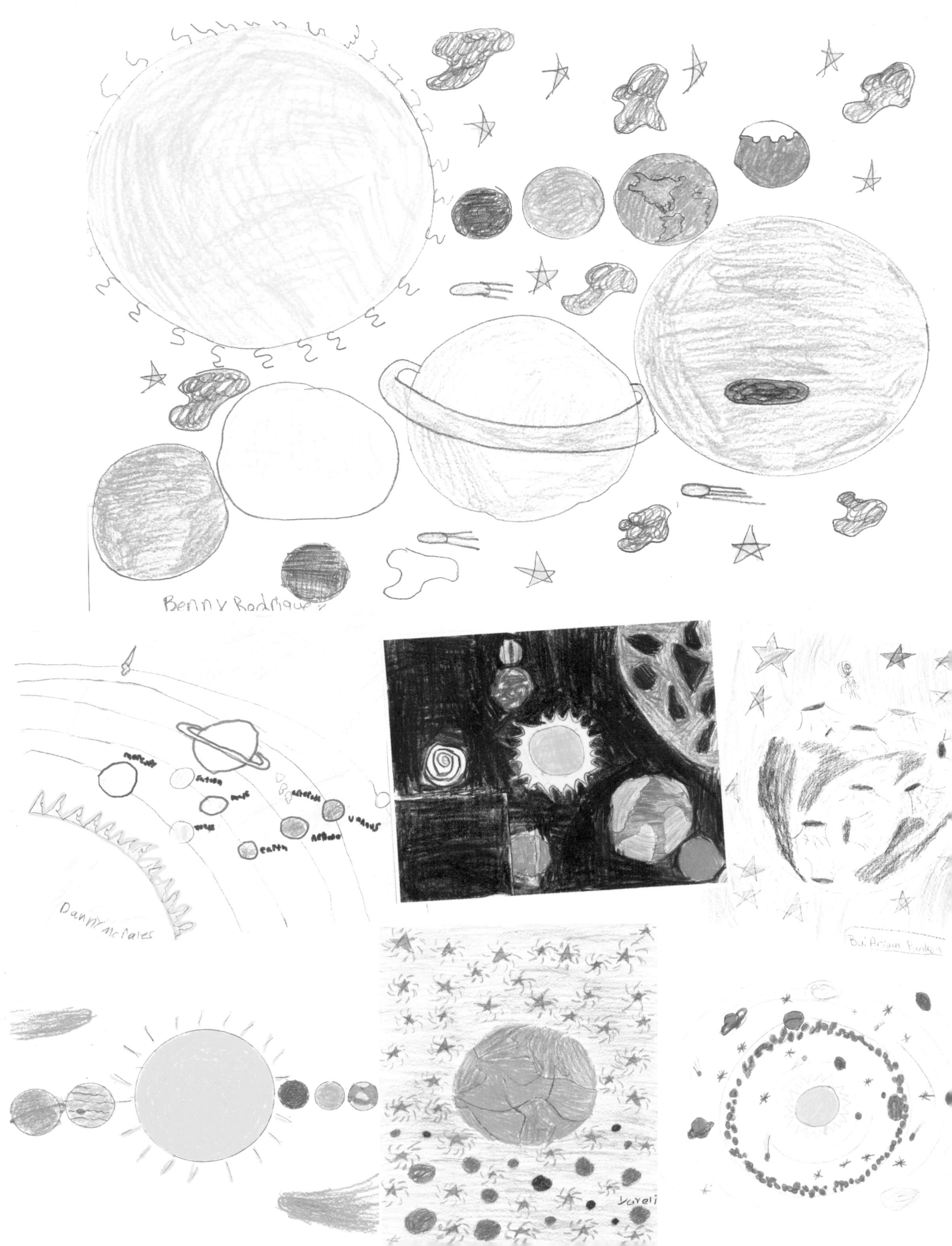

Benny Rodriquez
earth
Yareli

# Astronomy: the Solar System

Written and Illustrated by: April Chloe Terrazas

This book is dedicated to:

My Super Awesome Cousins

Jimito & Mike Ruiz

Through y'all, I have truly been able to reach for the stars!

Astronomy: The Solar System. April Chloe Terrazas, BS University of Texas at Austin.


Visit us on the web! www.Crazy-Brainz.com

Cover design, illustrations and text by: April Chloe Terrazas

## Some super cool terms to know:

# Orbit

Sound it Out

1. OR
2. BIT

The curved path of an object in space around a star, planet or moon. Do you see the moon orbiting Earth?

# Planet

Sound it Out

1. PLAN
2. IT

A large object in space that orbits around a star (like the Sun).
Do you see planet Earth?

# Crater

A large bowl-shaped area on the surface of a planet or moon. It is usually caused by an explosion or impact of a meteorite. Do you see the craters on the moon?

Sound it Out

1. KRA
2. TER

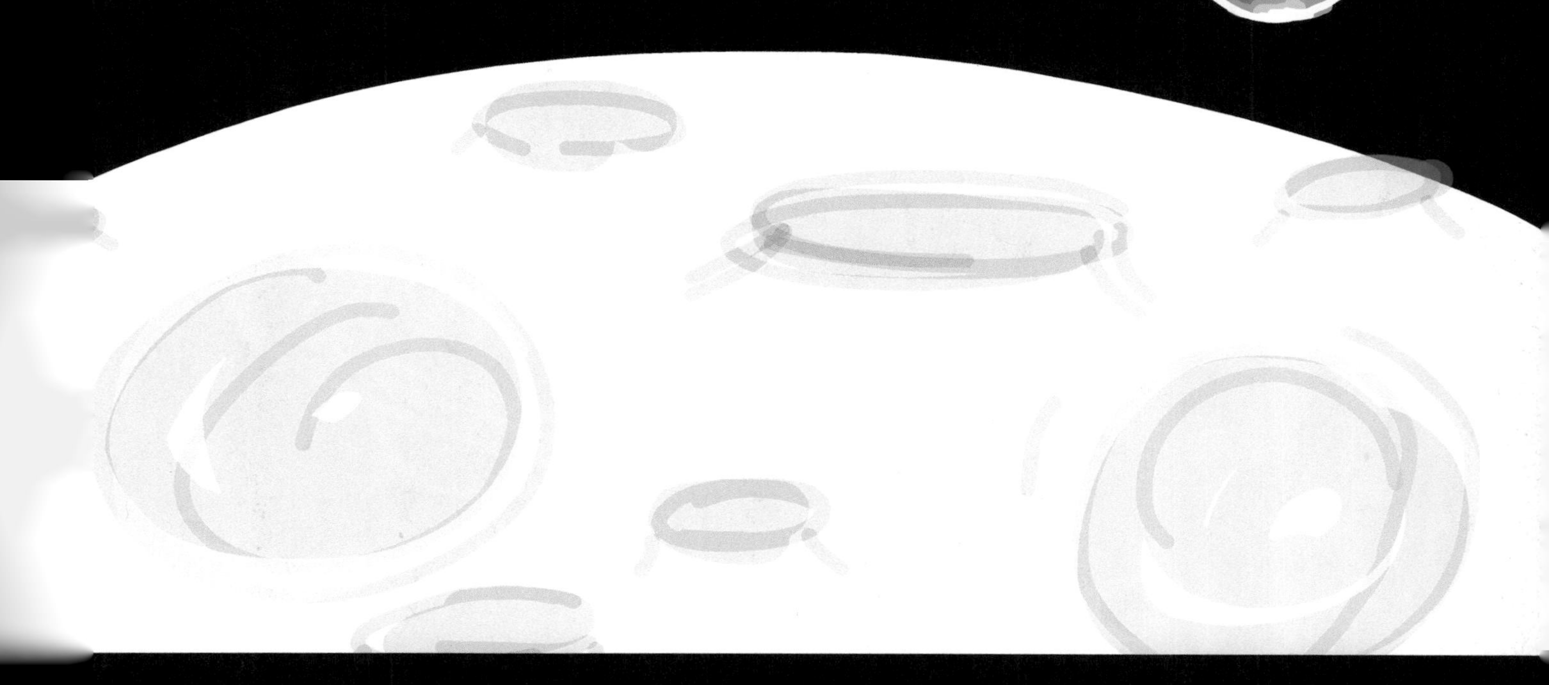

# Atmosphere

Sound it Out

1. AT
2. MUS
3. FEER

The gases surrounding a planet .
Oxygen and nitrogen are gases in Earth's atmosphere.

# Solar System

| Sound it Out |
| --- |
| 1. SO |
| 2. LAR |

| Sound it Out |
| --- |
| 1. SIS |
| 2. TEM |

All of this and more is in our Solar System.

The **Solar System** is the **Sun** and everything that **orbits** around it.

The **Sun** is the center of the **Solar System**.

What do you think **orbits** around the **Sun**?

**Sun**

Sound it Out

1. SUN

The **Sun** is a star.
A star is a big ball of hot gases that makes light and heat.

The **Sun** in our **Solar System** makes life on **Earth** possible.

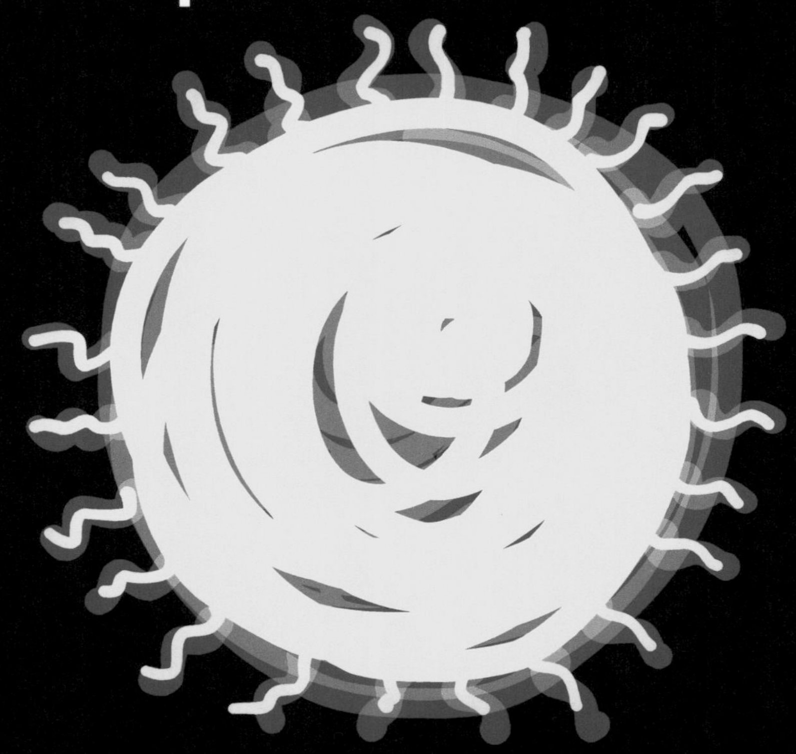

What does it feel like when the **Sun** is out? What does it feel like when the **Sun** is behind a cloud?

The **Sun** is a very common type of star in the **Milky Way Galaxy**.

# Milky Way Galaxy

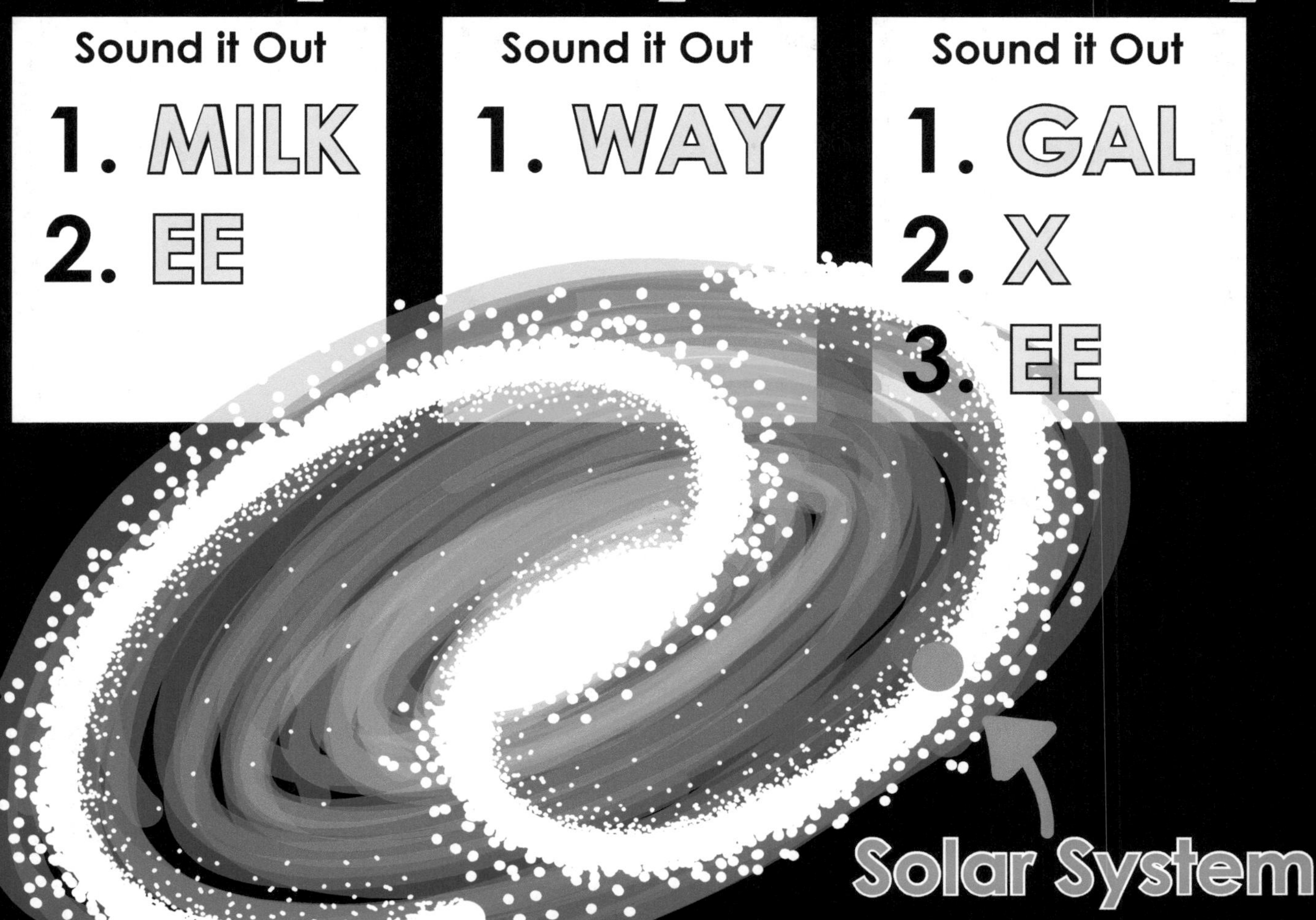


The **Milky Way Galaxy** is VERY BIG! Do you see the bright stars in the sky at night? ALL of those stars are in the **Milky Way Galaxy**!

Our **Solar System** is a *very small part* of the **Milky Way Galaxy**.

# Solar System: #1 MERCURY

Sound it Out

1. MUR
2. KU
3. REE

Mercury

The first planet
from the Sun is Mercury.

Mercury is 36 million miles from the Sun.

Mercury is the smallest planet in the Solar System. It is only a little bigger than our moon. It also looks like our moon. It is a solid surface that is covered with craters.

Mercury's very thin atmosphere contains the elements hydrogen, oxygen, sodium and helium.

Elements are discussed in *Chemistry: The Atom and Elements*, Book 2 of the Super Smart Science Series™.

*What is atmosphere?*

*What is a crater?*

# Solar System: #2 VENUS

| Sound it Out |
| --- |
| 1. VEE |
| 2. NUS |

# Venus

The second planet from the Sun is Venus.

Venus is 67 million miles from the Sun.

**The atmosphere around Venus contains the elements nitrogen and carbon dioxide.**

**Venus spins backwards compared to other planets!**

*What is the name of the first planet from the **Sun**?*

# Solar System: #3 EARTH

Sound it Out

1. ERTH

# Earth

The third planet
from the Sun is Earth.

Earth is 93 million miles from the Sun.

# Solar System: #3 EARTH

Earth is very special.
70% of Earth is covered with water, making it different from other planets in the Solar System.

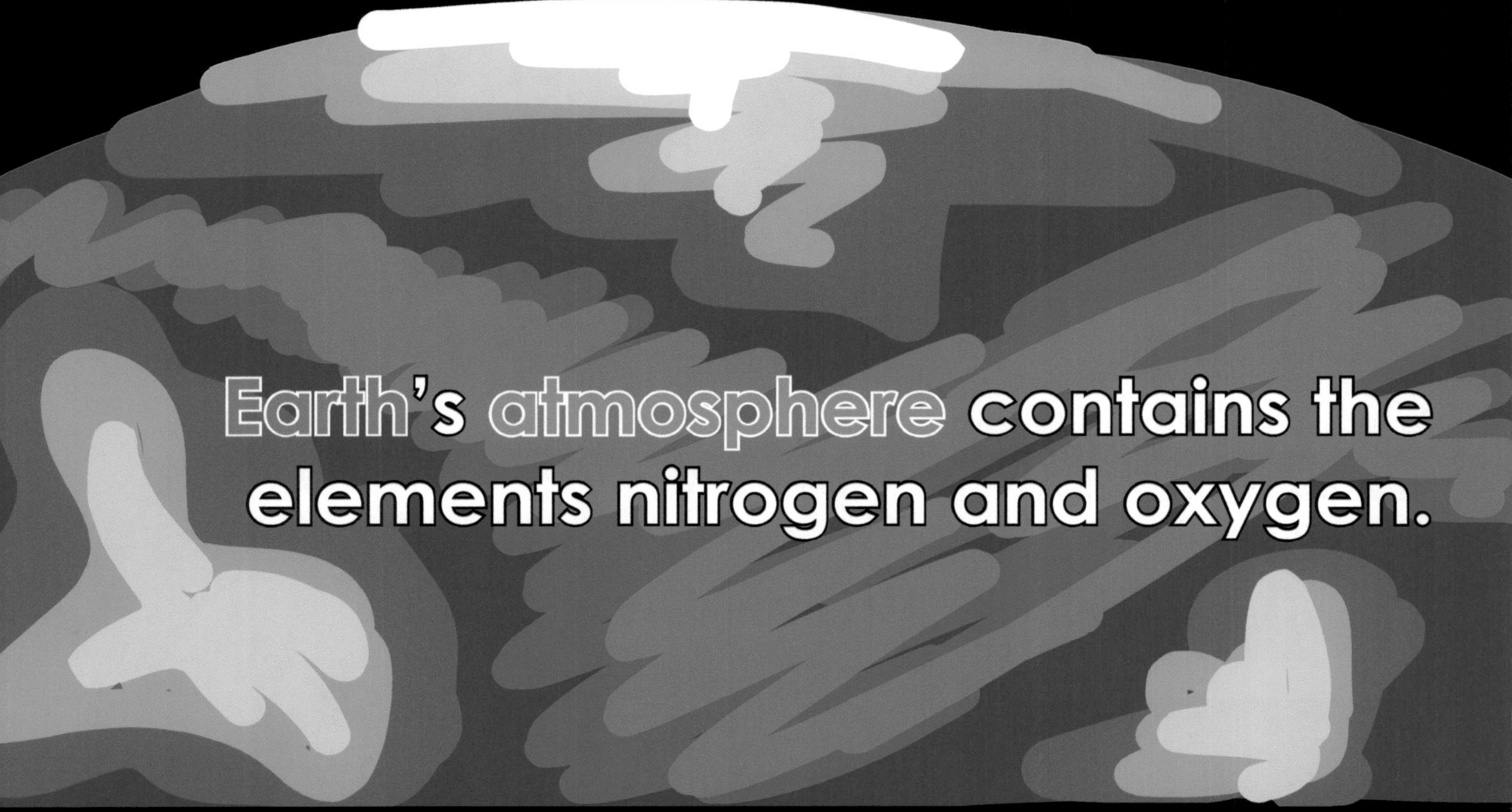

Earth's atmosphere contains the elements nitrogen and oxygen.

The land surface of Earth has mountains, canyons, valleys and flat land.

*What do you know about Earth?*

# Solar System: #4 MARS

The fourth planet
from the Sun is Mars.

Mars is 228 million miles from the Sun.

## Solar System: #4 MARS

**Mars is like a cold desert. Mars is similar to Earth because it has seasons, polar caps and varied land surfaces.**

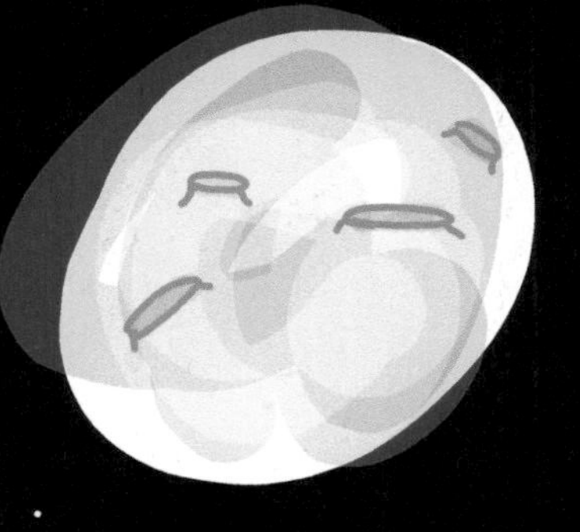

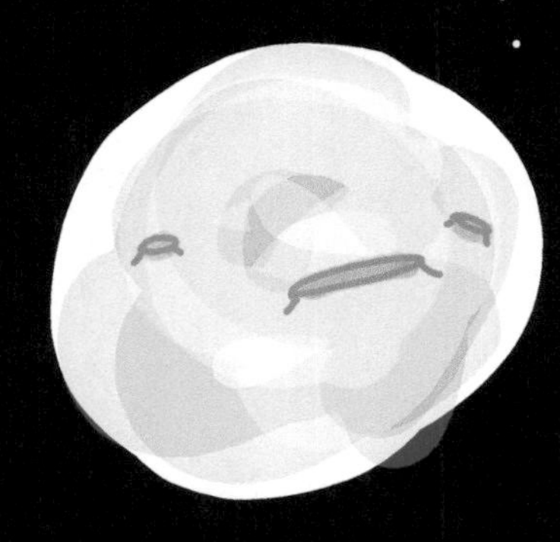

**Mars has TWO moons!**

**The atmosphere around Mars contains the elements carbon dioxide and nitrogen.**

*What are the first 3 planets from the **Sun**?*

*Which planet is covered mostly by water?*

Sound it Out

1. JU
2. PEH
3. TER

# Jupiter

The fifth planet from the Sun is Jupiter.

Jupiter is the BIGGEST planet in the Solar System.

Jupiter is 484 million miles from the Sun.

# Solar System: #5 JUPITER

**Jupiter has many moons, over 50!**

**There is a HUGE storm called the *Great Red Spot* that has existed for hundreds of years! (It is so big that 3 Earth's can fit inside!)**

**Jupiter's atmosphere contains hydrogen and helium.**

**Jupiter is not like the first 4 planets because it is a gas-giant planet. It does NOT have a solid surface.**

*What are the first 5 planets from the **Sun**?*

# Solar System: #6 SATURN

**Sound it Out**

1. SA
2. TURN

# Saturn

The sixth **planet** from the **Sun** is **Saturn**.

**Saturn** is 886 million miles from the **Sun**.

# Solar System: #6 SATURN

**Saturn** is unique because of its 7 fantastic rings that are made of ice and rock.

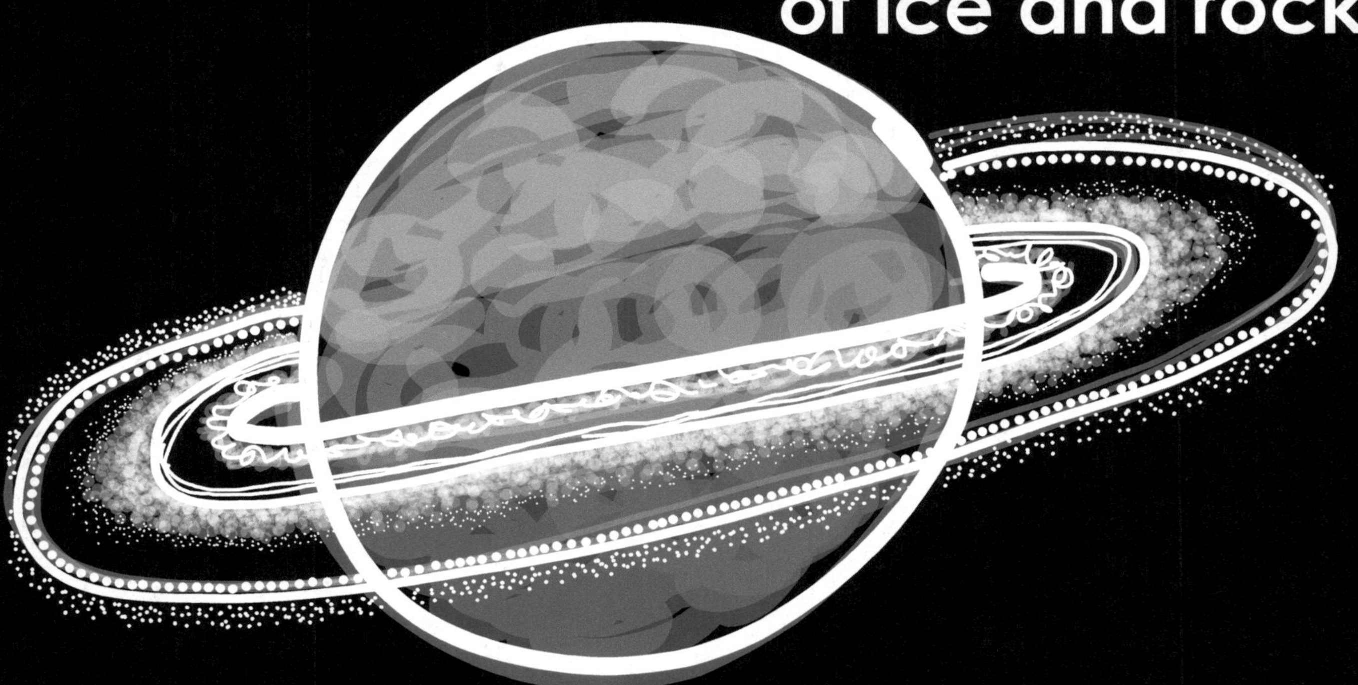

**Saturn**'s **atmosphere** contains hydrogen and helium.

**Saturn**, like **Jupiter**, is a gas-giant and has over 50 moons.

*What is the name of the HUGE storm on **Jupiter**?*

# Solar System: #7 URANUS

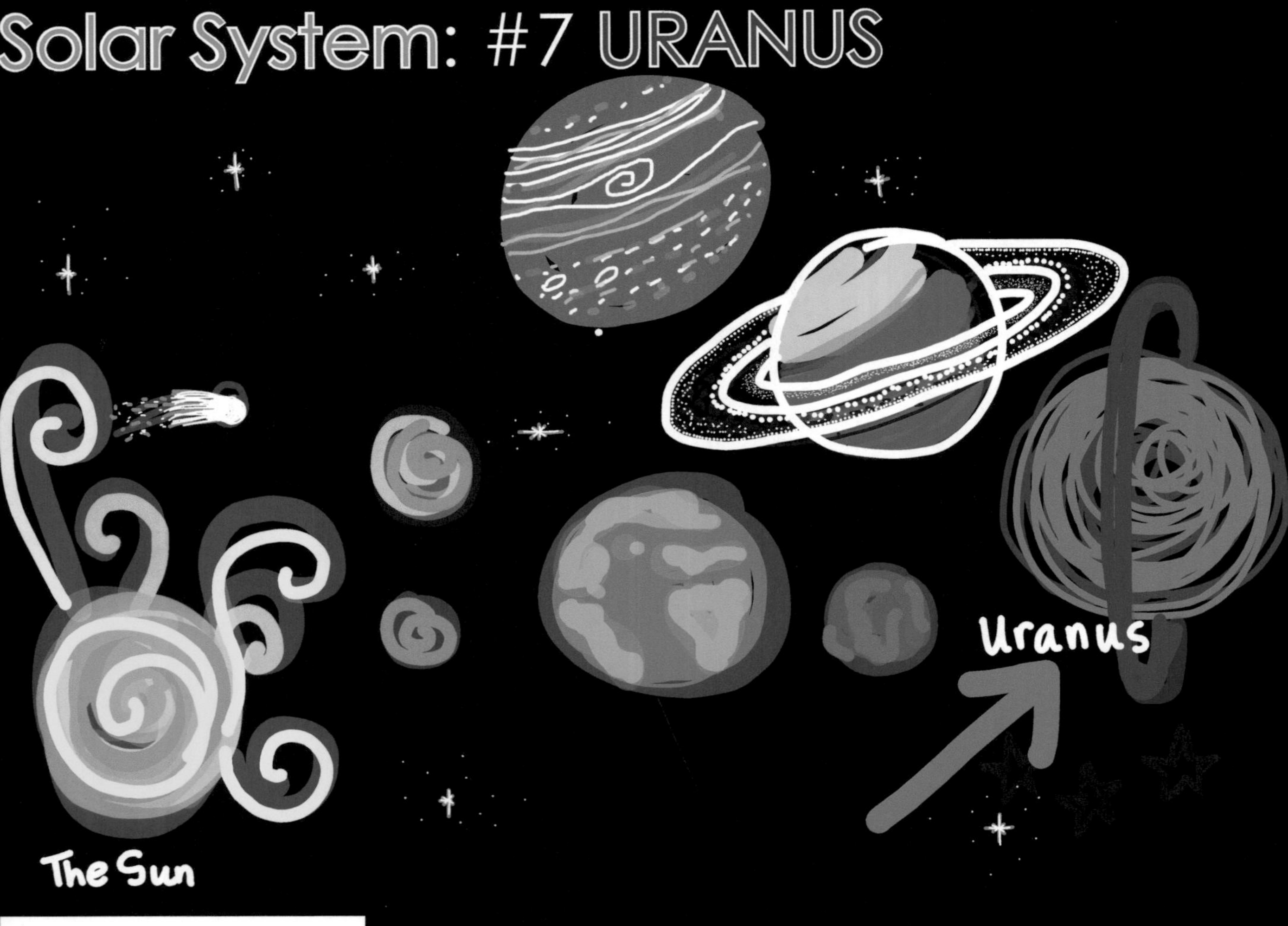


| Sound it Out |
| --- |
| 1. UR |
| 2. A |
| 3. NUS |

# Uranus

The seventh planet from the Sun is Uranus.

Uranus is 1.8 billion miles from the Sun.

# Solar System: #7 URANUS

A molecule called methane gives Uranus its blue color.

Uranus has 13 rings.

Uranus is a gas-giant.

The atmosphere of Uranus contains hydrogen and helium.

Uranus spins backwards!

*What other planet spins backwards*?

# Solar System: #8 NEPTUNE

Sound it Out

1. NEP
2. TOON

# Neptune

The eighth planet
from the Sun is Neptune.

Neptune is 2.8 billion miles from the Sun.

Neptune is the farthest planet from the Sun in the Solar System.

Neptune's atmosphere contains hydrogen and helium.

Neptune is a gas-giant.

*What other planets are gas-giants?*

*Can you name all of the planets beginning closest to the Sun?*

# QUIZ

What planets are gas-giants?

What is the closest planet to the Sun in the Solar System?

What is the farthest planet from the Sun in the Solar System?

Which planets spin backwards?

What is the name of the HUGE storm on Jupiter?

The Solar System is in what Galaxy?

# TRUE OR FALSE?

70% of Earth is covered by water.

Saturn has less than 5 moons.

Neptune has 13 rings.

The Sun is the center
of the Solar System.

Uranus is blue because of
oxygen in the atmosphere.

# What else is in the Solar System other than planets and the Sun?

## Dwarf Planet

| Sound it Out | Sound it Out |
| --- | --- |
| 1. DWRF | 1. PLAN<br>2. IT |

Dwarf planets orbit the Sun. Dwarf planets are much smaller than regular planets and can be found farther out past Neptune. Pluto is a dwarf planet.

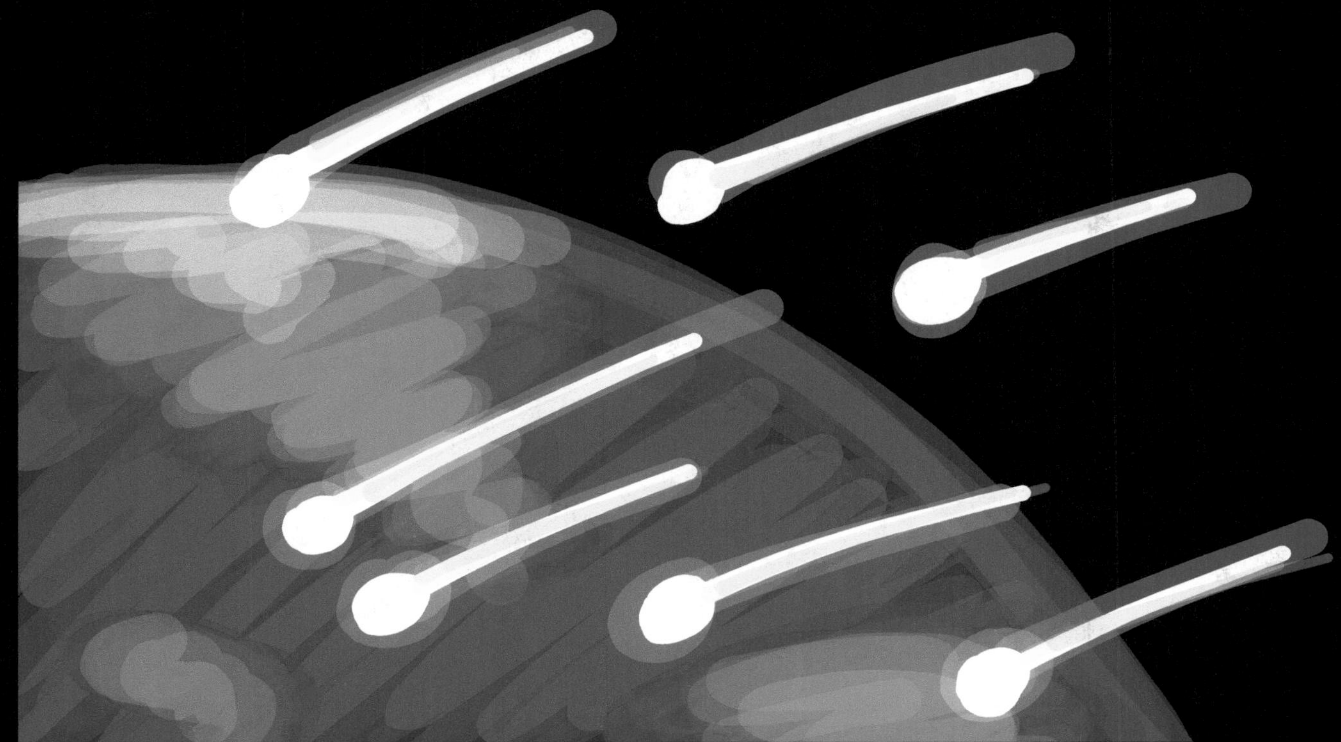

# Meteors and Meteorites

**Sound it Out**

1. MEE
2. TEE
3. OR

**Sound it Out**

1. MEE
2. TEE
3. OR
4. ITE

Meteors are made of rock. As meteors enter Earth's atmosphere, they become shooting stars! Meteorites are meteors that go through the atmosphere and hit the land surface of a planet.

Asteroids are pieces of rock that orbit the Sun. There is a large area called the Asteroid Belt between Mars and Jupiter where there are millions of asteroids!

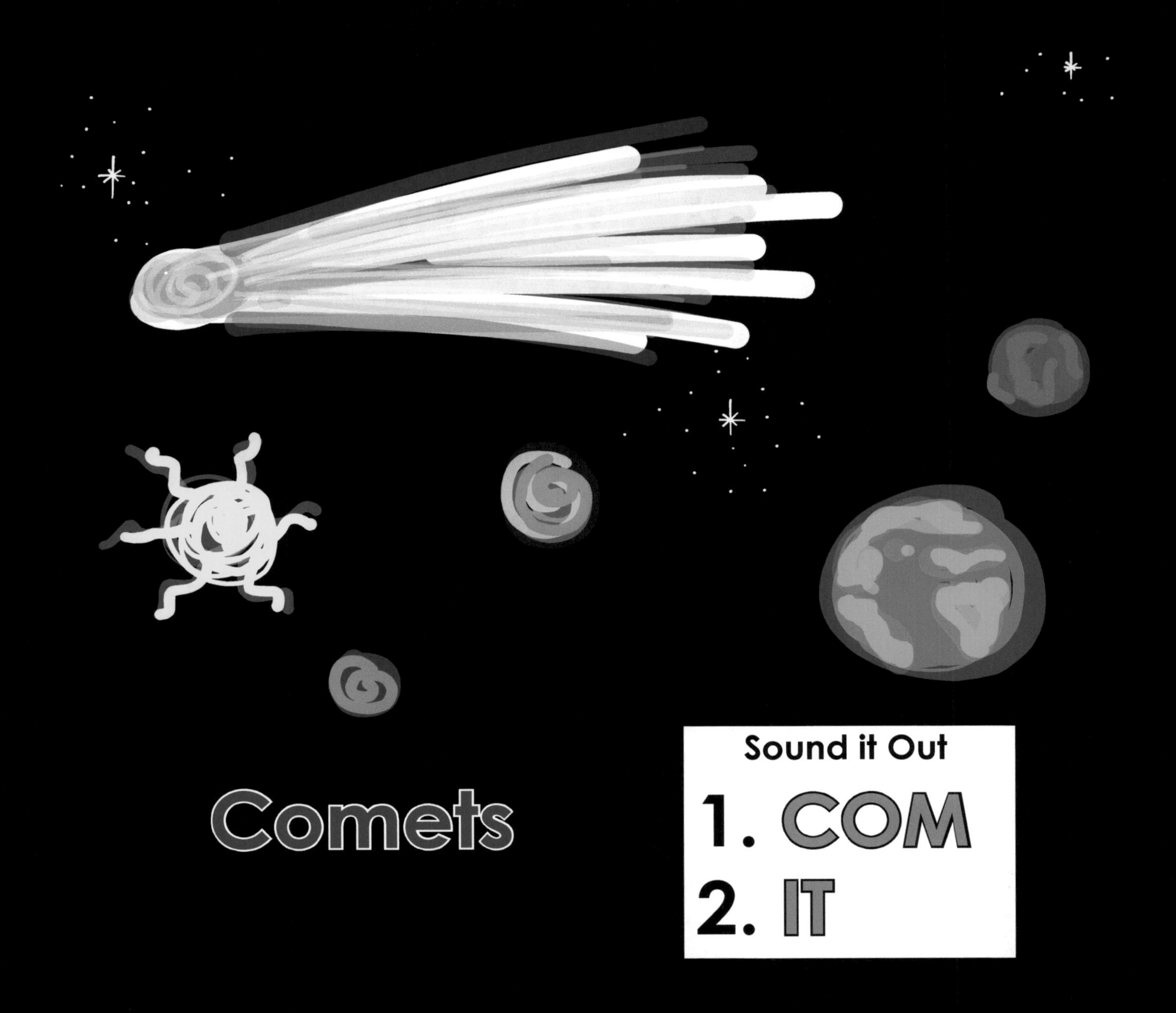

# Comets

Sound it Out

1. COM
2. IT

Comets are big frozen balls of rock and gases. When a comet gets close to the Sun, it gets hot and creates a large glowing ball with a very long tail that you can sometimes see from Earth!

# The Solar System is AMAZING!

## A person who studies the Solar System is called an Astronomer.

## Astronomer

Sound it Out

1. AH
2. STRON
3. O
4. MER

## Telescope

Sound it Out

1. TEL
2. EH
3. SKOP

## Satellite

Sound it Out

1. SAT
2. EL
3. LITE

Telescope

Satellite

Astronomers look through telescopes and see far out in space. They also monitor satellites that send information back to Earth.

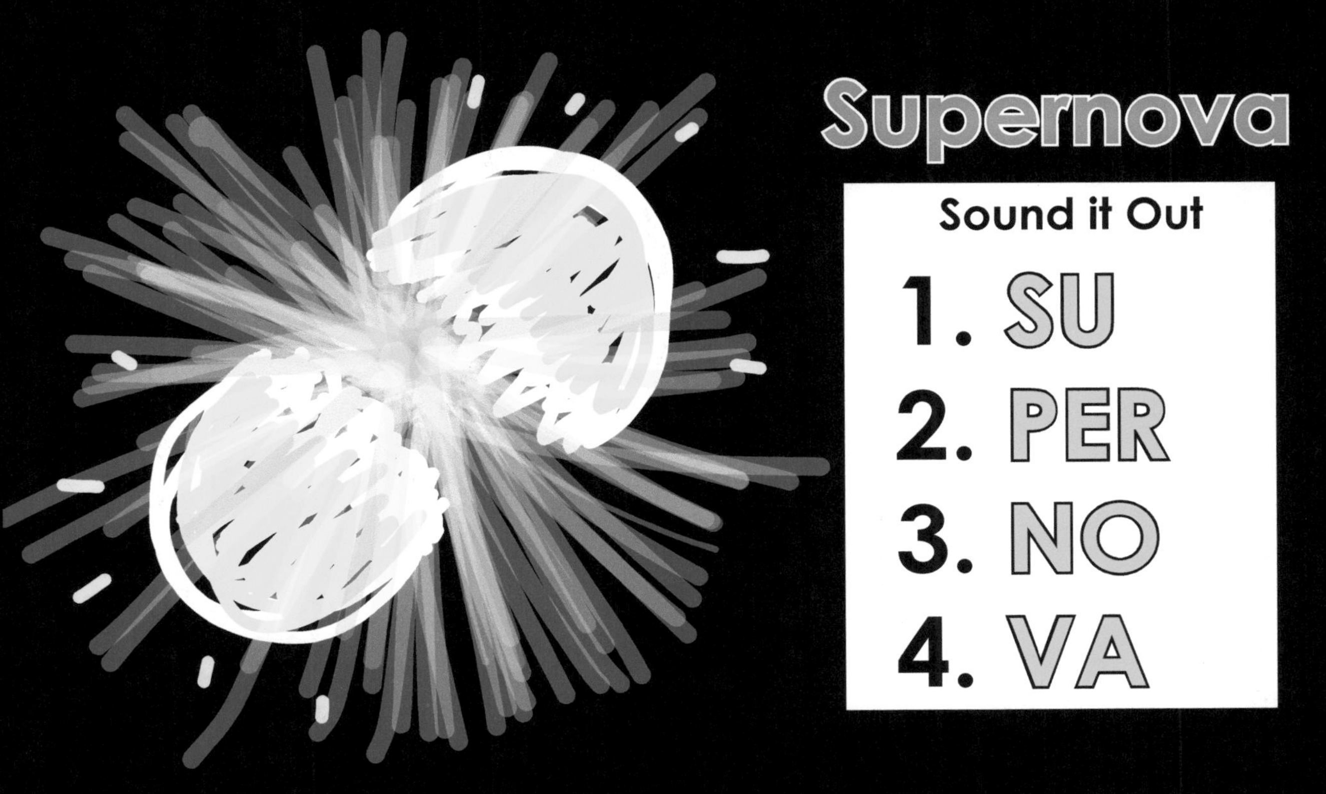


Astronomers see very interesting things in space, like supernovas. A supernova is an exploding star!

They can even see farther out into the Milky Way Galaxy past the Solar System!

The Solar System is an exciting place where 8 planets orbit the Sun.

Each planet has elements in the atmosphere.

Some planets have a land surface, some planets are gas-giants.

In the Solar System there are also Dwarf Planets, Meteors, Asteroids and Comets.

The Solar System is only a small part of the Milky Way Galaxy.

Astronomers look through telescopes and use satellites to explore stars, planets and supernovas everyday!

## *Review the terms you learned!*

Solar System
Sun
Planet
Crater
Atmosphere
Orbit
Mercury
Venus
Earth
Mars
Dwarf Planet
Asteroid
Jupiter
Supernova
Telescope
Saturn
Uranus
Neptune
Satellite
Astronomer
Milky Way Galaxy
Meteor
Comet

# Create your own planet!

## What is it called? Does it have moons?
## Where is it located in the Solar System?
## What elements are in the atmosphere?
## Does it have rings?

***<u>Draw it here</u>:***

CPSIA information can be obtained
at www.ICGtesting.com
Printed in the USA
BVHW020935110819
555522BV00010B/274/P

*9780991147205*